Copyright © 2020
Remilekun Kehinde-Philip

40 LIFE LESSONS

ISBN: 978-978-985-361-8

Published by:
Mind Shift Series Academy (MSSA)

+234 813 501 6551, +234 706 441 6283

Layout Design:
AyanfeOluwa Publishing Services (APS)
+2347089203076
info@coachayanfeoluwa.com
www.coachayanfeoluwa.com

Dedication

This book is dedicated to everyone who, at one point in their journey, experienced some level of pain but came out triumphantly with the help of God.

Also to all the 40 widows that will be getting 50% of the proceeds from the sale of this book on the launch date.

Acknowledgements

With reference to Isaiah 50:4-5, my favourite scripture, my gratitude goes to God Almighty, the Game Changer and my Creator, who is the inspiration behind the idea of writing this piece. I am thankful to the One who blesses the works of my hands for all the life experience that has shaped me into the person I am today.

I am particularly thankful to Sola Adesakin, my finance coach, who, through her numerous teachings, has influenced my business acumen and financial journey.

To my ever-loving parents, Pastor and Pastor (Mrs.) Olujimi Olusola Obadina, I am forever grateful to God for bringing me out of your loins. I thank God for preserving you to see me become and attain this milestone. I appreciate all your sacrifices, never-ending support and love.

My darling sister, Toluwalope Obadina, thank you for your unrelenting effort in putting the manuscript together. You have always been so supportive, my aburo.

To all my former colleagues at BD Consult and Chain Reactions, I celebrate you all. To Aunty Ekaete Enang, a true big sister of many years, thank you for listening to me when I discussed the idea of writing a memoir with you some days after the passing of Pastor Ibidun Ighodalo.

To all my clients on all my social media platforms, and everyone within my network who constantly reacts on my content and send feedback, this book will not be complete without you.

My inner circle sisters, I celebrate you all and for the bond so strong that we all share.

To my husband, Dee as I fondly call you and my children, Oluwatamilore and Tirenioluwa, you guys are super awesome. Thank you for supporting mummy. You are indeed my superheroes!

I appreciate my Pastor Sam and Nike Adeyemi, who have set my mind on fire by being part of the Daystar family, which they founded together.

To my Pastor and his wife, Pastor Seyi and Wunmi Oluseye, you sure know me inside out. Thank you for your calls and support at all times.

Thank you, Mrs. Adedolapo Ebadan, for making out time to edit this work and offer advice as and when necessary.

To all my destiny helpers - praying clients, paying clients, support system, Daystar family, old and new friends, I am grateful for the gift of you.

To Dr. Tunde Ogunsina, Dr. Ibikunle, Daddy Feyisitan and all staff members of Hossanah Specialist Hospital, Ilaro, I am deeply grateful for standing by me during those trying years.

To my Uncles and Aunties, Peter and Foluke Oyeneye, Gboyega & Yemi Oyeneye, Jola and Funke Oyeneye, Michael and Rose Oyeneye, Funto & Koyejo Obadina, Funmi, Femi & Sola Feyisitan, Yemi Obadina, Uncle Dele Obadina, Biola Ewetade, you all have contributed to my life at one point or the other and for this, I am super grateful.

To Ven. (Dr.) and Mrs Olukoyejo Oduola Obadina, thank you for your love and care. To former Honorable Commissioner for physical planning and urban developmet Tpl. Toyin Ayinde and wife, Mrs. Rhoda Ayinde, Mummy Fayemi (My God mother), Pastor & Pastor Mrs. Chapi, Mrs. Temitope Abibu(Nee Mokuolu), Mrs. Fola Osasona, Mrs Mojisola Edun and Bro. Kunle Gab, I am super grateful for all your love and support.

Finally, to you reading this book, thank you for deeming it fit to get your copy.

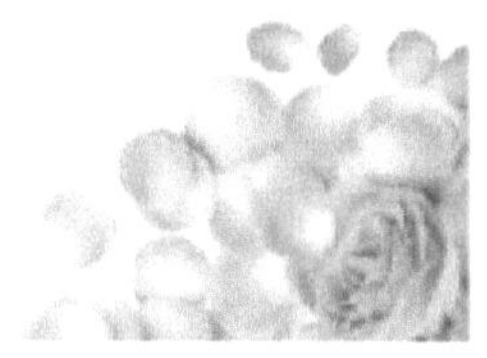

Foreword

This book is a laudable attempt by the author, Mrs Remilekun Kehinde-Philip, to allow the reader have a look into her professional life and also part of her private life, especially, the aspects which have to do with goal setting, entrepreneurship, commitment, courage, continuous improvement, overcoming trials and faith in God. It is only a person with the heart of gold and the love for societal well-being who will open up her life so much to the reading public. I salute the courage of the author.

As early as 2001 when Remi relocated to Jos, Plateau State, for her academic pursuit, I had noticed some unique attributes about her- her love for books, gifts, writing, public speaking, productivity, entrepreneurship, planning skills and prayer.

I'm excited that the young Remi has now become a thought leader, influencer, public speaker, trainer, serial entrepreneur and now an author. Whenever we discuss, I see a person thinking and speaking above her age. This tells me Remi's stint at the Nigeria Institute of Journalism (NIJ), Nigerian Institute of Public Relations (NIPR) and Pan African University was not in vain. Added to that are her winning spirit, personal efforts, support of family and friends and above all the special grace of God.

I'm too convinced Mrs Kehinde-Philip won't stop writing just after this book. There are many books in her. She is too loaded with ideas and thoughts that need to be expressed so that people of this generation and the next will be adequately blessed and inspired by her.

This book will definitely cause a revolution among young people and much older professionals because through it you will see raw courage, positive mindset, power of relationship, learning outside of the four walls of school, business skills, new ideas and faith in God which you can apply to life situations.

With about 33 years of Public Relations practice experience behind me, when I see a good product I can recognise it. I therefore recommend this book to young people, youth leaders, professionals and business executives. Besides picking your own copy, please, be charitable enough to give one or two copies to friends and persons in your neighbourhood, church or office.

Thanks and God bless.

Peter Oyeneye, PhD., fnipr
CEO, Advanced Management Academy
Abuja.

Book Review

BOOK REVIEW

What a joy to write a review for my dearest friend and sister -Remilekun Kehinde-Philip (Rem-Rem). It is such great pride to see how she has flourished and thrived as she has in the last 40years.

Remi and I were colleagues in a public relations firm; while initial interaction with her was that of a shy, self-absorbed, unsmiling young woman, one thing I could not overlook was the efficiency and reliability she brought to her work. Remi is such a powerhouse; the steel-like resilience that she brings to bear has been forged by experiences and one that posterity will judge her fairly for detailing in this book.

We cannot fully enjoy life learning from our mistakes alone; we never live long enough. That is why we study and engage the experiences of other people to help us along with this once in a lifetime journey to avoid certain pitfalls, reduce our errors and embrace traits that can help us live a more rewarding and successful life.

This book reflects all of us. You will encounter human frailty, reliance on God, the benefits of trusted and supportive circles, the need for repositioning for growth, and the responsibility to self. The success evident in Remi's life through Grace, innovation, hard work, and adaptability to change is a timely reminder that we can succeed in our lives as she charges us to be all we can positively be.

As Remi has urged us by the documentation of her 40 years memoir, be thankful for your journey and continue to thrive.

Thank you for sharing, Rem-Rem!
Florence Ozor

I could not find enough words to appreciate this noble sense of thought that has been accurately written; so, I summarily arrived at tagging it "Timely Renaissance". This is quite an unavoidable dairy that should be passed from one generation to another.

Pastor Olujimi Olushola Obadina (My Dad)

I thoroughly enjoyed reading this book, 40 LIFE LESSONS that has been thoroughly captured by the author, Remilekun Kehinde-Philip. From the very first moment I started reading the Book I did not stop till I got to the end. The writing is brilliantly articulated; it transformed me into the author's world and captured every vital element of her experience in very precise yet relatable detail. Reading this book gave me the feeling I get when I watch a really good movie and know that I would want to watch the movie again and still experience the same level of intrigue I experienced at first watch. True to my prediction, I had an amazing time when I read the book the second time; every word jumped out at me like I was reading the book for the first time.

It is indeed a beautifully written and truly inspirational read which I would recommend for everyone looking for titbits and nuggets on life lessons. I am very proud and honored to have been chosen by the author to review this book.

My very best wishes, Remilekun Kehinde-Philip

Yetunde Falade
Director, Corporate Affairs and Marketing
Pineapple TV

What a joy and a privilege to be asked to write a Book Review for the book authored by a woman of remarkable courage, candour and compassion.

Remi was in the team that accompanied Sola Adesakin, the lead coach of Smart Stewards, to a Women Conference held in my church, in which Sola was

facilitating. At the round table where I hosted Sola and her team; in the course of the conversation, Remi chipped in that she sells shoes and somehow, the statement was etched in my memory. I was particularly impressed with how she comported herself, yet seized the opportunity to pitch her enterprise without being obtrusive. Not too long after, my daughter needed a pair of shoes and I reverted to her and have been doing so since then without regret. I recall at one time, as a result of poor network, her account was credited thrice for the same purchase and she immediately reversed and refunded the value to me without delay. Such integrity is rare to come by these days.

On this your special and auspicious milestone, I pray for you that the blessings of the Lord upon your life will be made manifest in every facet of your life; the next forty years will launch you the more in the emptying of your gifting to the world that God has called you to impact. I invoke upon you, the covenant of longevity and I decree that you shall live long and strong and see your desires over your children in Jesus' powerful name.
Congratulations and a very Happy Birthday!

I have heard people say **"Life begins at 40"**
I believe life begins the moment you access and apply knowledge that activates and enhances the quality of your life. It is therefore in your best interest to access such relevant knowledge early enough to live your life with purpose and passion. That is what the book **40 Life**

Lessons has achieved very succinctly. It has made available, valuable lessons needed to transit from a life of mediocrity to a life on a mission, from a place of pain to a place of purpose.

The book is a compendium of wisdom nuggets, drawn from the author's personal experiences, to fuel one to thrust forward in life and wrestle oneself free from internal storms and by the same storm soar high to unimaginable heights that conquer personal fears and limitations.

Remilekun has skillfully crafted in her book, the intricate balance of fighting personal wars with external expectations and yet coming out victorious in it all, leaving memories that serve as a springboard for impacting others.

2 Corinthians 1:3-4 AMP
Blessed [gratefully praised and adored] be the God and Father of our Lord Jesus Christ, the Father of mercies and the God of all comfort, who comforts and encourages us in every trouble so that we will be able to comfort and encourage those who are in any kind of trouble, with the comfort with which we ourselves are comforted by God.

Remilekun is impacting lives now, by the comfort and encouragement she has received from the Lord. Indeed, she is a woman helped by God.

I highly recommend this book to anyone that desires to live a life of impact, a life of transition from ashes to beauty and a life of victory over all…a life helped by God.

Pastor Mrs. Harriet O. Olubiyo
Triumphant Christian Centre, Lagos
Email: pastor@harrietolubiyo.org
www.harrietolubiyo.org

40 Life Lessons is indeed a story of a lady helped by God. In this memoir, we see a lady who life has dealt some blows, but who came out of the tunnel brighter, better and positively impacting the world around her. It touches Remilekun's journey at various stages of her life such that you will be encouraged to live a life of total dependence on God.

I always admire the doggedness and loyalty of Remilekun to the Smart Stewards Vision as she's one person you can be sure will accompany Sola Adesakin to her speaking engagements. This, no doubt resonated with Life Lesson 17 where she dwelt on her love for supporting people and adding value, something she does constantly and effortlessly.

I will recommend this book to anyone who is at a crossroad, tired, feeling life should have more to offer, for them to know that there is hope, and generally for everyone to know that God is nearer than we think and that His grace is available to bring out the best in us even as He has done with Remilekun, polishing her into the shining and beautiful star that we all know now.

Mrs. Folashade Kola-Eke

40 **LIFE LESSONS** by Remilekun Kehinde-Philip is a confirmation of the statement "Behind every glory, there is a story".

Remi, a determined, resilient, dedicated, and delectable entrepreneur has given back herself to all who want to move from nothing to something. Her courage in putting her story together and love for the needy to decide to give half of the income from the book to 40 widows is commendable.

The simplicity of the language and brevity of the lessons/chapters make the book an easy read.

I recommend the book to all who think they have come to the end of the road, all who want to start a business, and those who have always thought writing a book is a herculean task or impossibility.

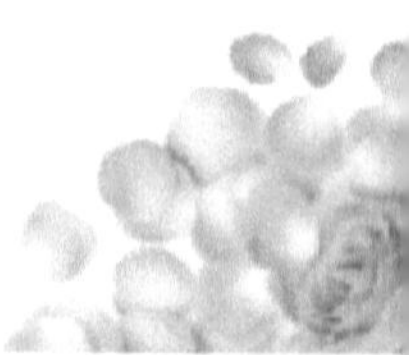

It will spur you on.
Now is the time. Don't give up on your dreams.

Mrs. Rhoda Ayinde
Public Administrator of repute, Mentor, Marriage counselor, and retired Permanent Secretary of Lagos State Government.

There are no "self-made" men anywhere; every man is "helper-made," and the source of the help can either be human or divine. Like David said in Psalm 121:1-2 (TPT), "I look up to the mountains and hills, longing for God's help. But realize that our true help and protection come only from the Lord, our Creator who made the heavens and the earth".

Indeed, it is evident that Remilekun has enjoyed God's help that activates human assistance and favor. Her openness and emotional connection shine through in the simple language and writing style that makes this book easy to read for all.

We all face different challenges in life but coming out victorious and vibrant requires not allowing oneself to be limited by such challenges. This lesson is clearly reflected in several parts of the book.

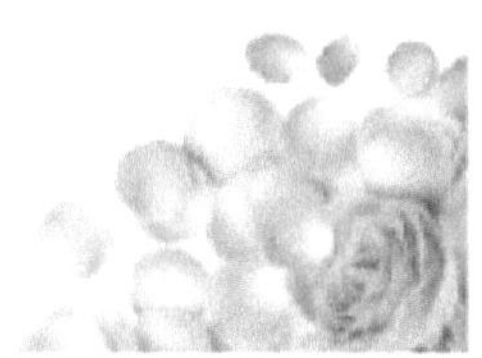

I recommend this book to everyone as a guide or a reminder that life's journey is not smooth all through. As one trusts and holds on to God for each phase, one will surely come out triumphantly scaling through the walls. I look forward to the Mind Shift Series.

Omowunmi Oluwaseye

Remi has poured her life's experiences into this book as a way of encouraging readers. Her resilience and go-getter spirit is on display as she shares her stories. The universe rewards those who take action and this is evidenced by all she has been able to accomplish so far. I believe this is just the beginning of greater things ahead. Congratulations.

Sola Adesakin
Lead Coach & Founder, Smart Stewards

I would love to congratulate Remilekun for this great work and also for the courage to teach and encourage others, using her life experiences through this book.

40 is one of those ages that everyone; maybe most women, look forward to celebrating.

This could be because from a spiritual standpoint, the number 40 is often related to signify the end of a cycle; as it was with Jesus in the wilderness having fasted for 40 days and 40 nights. We also see that God made the Israelites wander in the wilderness for 40 years. And so, when we come into this age, it is spiritually significant that one has come into a new season of spiritual renewal and can begin to walk in the fullness of the manifestation of their calling.

The lessons in this book are from raw experiences from the life of the author and she has carefully highlighted the high points of her life, albeit not all nice, revealing God at the centre of it all.

I recommend this book for people of all ages because it will prepare everyone who picks it up to live life and enjoy every moment even if they cannot wait to reach the significant age 40. And for those who have passed this age mark, each lesson is another opportunity being opened up to you so you can realize that your best life still lies ahead of you.

Pastor Bidemi Mark-Mordi

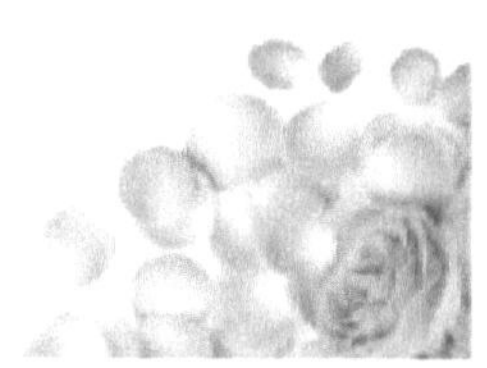

Contents

CONTENTS

Introduction

Growing up, I thought hitting the 40-year mark would take forever. I tread life's sacred path with the experience of each new day filling up my story that has become my glory today.

Some days were gloomy and long, while some nights stayed dark and brought no stars my way. Many times, my strength failed me as the tunnel did not promise light at its end. Yet, I held my head up and hoped for the best.

I fed on optimism as I grew and found my will. Light soon began to flood my path as I encountered the One who created me and proved to me in no small measure that I am truly the Father's beloved – a lady helped by God.

On my journey getting here, I picked up many lessons and as I celebrate this milestone, I am glad to share my memoir. The 40 life lessons shared in this book will help you reflect on your life, make you appreciate yourself and strengthen your resolve not to give up on life just yet.

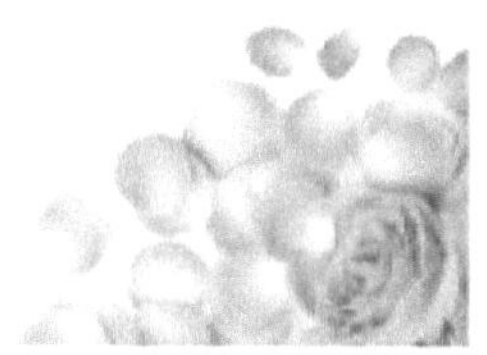

INTRODUCTION

The lessons have been kept short for your reading pleasure, bearing in mind that they will teach, intrigue, inspire, motivate and charge you to be better.

Have a great read as you welcome me to the big 40!

I celebrate me…

Life Lesson

1

DON'T WALK ALONE

Why walk alone? Life in itself is a lovely path/journey that requires people with whom you will navigate through. I used to be an introvert, enjoying my own company. Little did I know I was depriving myself of the great company of people who probably would have made my life and journey easier and faster. Tell me, can you actually walk alone? When you walk alone, you can only achieve a few things. But when you walk with the right people, it will amaze you how much more you can achieve within a short time. There are certain helpers you need in your life to quicken your purpose and help you navigate life fast enough. Be sure not to miss these people out of your decision to remain perpetually introverted.

Take away: You need the gift of Men! Men who will hold your hands, genuine circle of friends and community that are never ashamed of your growth, leaps and wins. Enough of solo runs! Move with like minds and shine your light unapologetically.

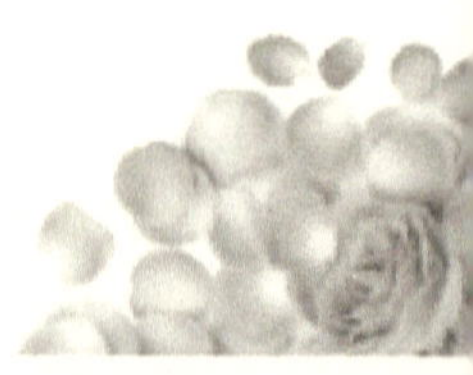

Life Lesson

2

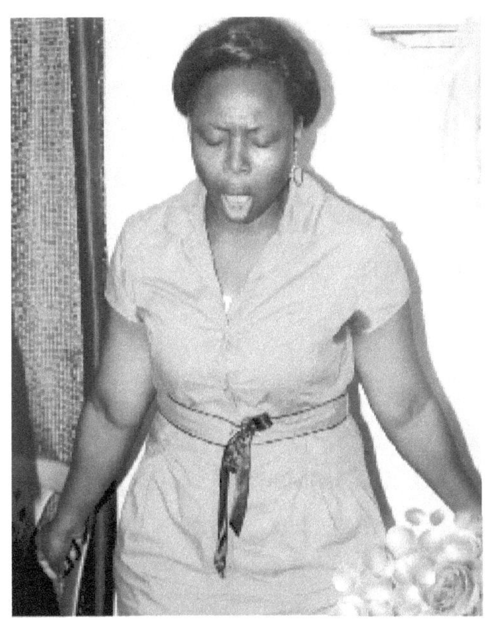

THE GOD-FACTOR

There is always the God-factor in this journey called life which we cannot overrule. I am an unrepentant lover of God. I have erred many times and I am not all perfect like some saints. But in every step of the way, I have learnt to acknowledge God in my journey. I never fail to ask God for every "next" step to take; and so, when exclamations are expressed at my achievements in life, I am always quick to attribute all to God. I understand so well how making God a part of my life works. So, I sometimes ask Him when I need to build my clientele base. Funny as it might sound, but it is that important. Those you allow in your space and those you do business with are very important to God and your growth process.

When I go on social media, my personal page, for instance, I deliberately involve God for guidance on my engagements.

Take away: The need to constantly engage God in our dealings can ease off stress and give more meaning and credibility to our daily activities. We can deliberately ride on the wings of grace. It is the supernatural factor that causes our life's results to surpass our human efforts.

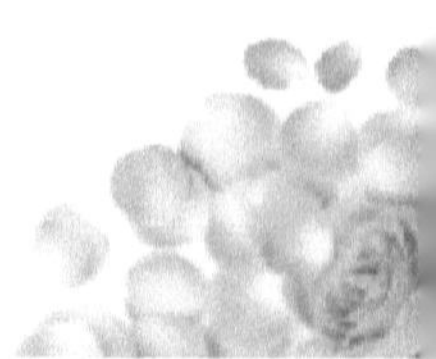

Life Lesson

3

THE WIDOW OF ZAREPHATH

There was a time in my life when I was heavily in debts running to the tune of N3 million, owing to a wrong investment. My life was shattered; as that amount seemed too much a cross for me to bear. I became a ghost of myself, to say the least. As much as I tried to retain my sanity, I lost my mind and sense of relationship. This spanned a while until a fateful day when I read about the widow of Zarephath again. In the light of the fresh revelation I got from that story, I took everything to God in prayer and opened up.

Truth is there will always be a time we feel all hope is lost and tend to accept low self-esteem. I got to a point when I had to believe that God could always mend our mess even when they are self-inflicted. However, the big question is: "What exactly do we have in our hands for God to multiply?"

Take away: A life of faith does not prevent affliction. However, we should be resolute in our resolve that God is mindful of us, while not forgetting that there is a part of us that should move the hand of God to action.

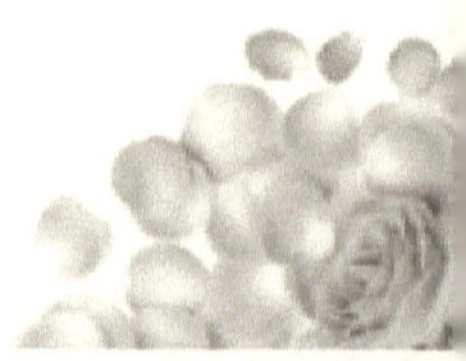

Life Lesson

4

DELAY IS NOT DENIAL

I had an ailment immediately after secondary school in 1997. For a whole year, I was in and out of the hospital. So, when others were transitioning into the higher institution of learning, I was a regular caller at hospitals, receiving treatment. Worse yet, I spent 6 straight months in the hospital. I lost hope and was living in self-pity and all, but God gave me a reassuring word through Bro. Kunle Gab. He sent me a copy of Bro. Gbile Akanni's Costly Assumption and wrote in one of the blank pages in the book: "Remi, you would suddenly wake up one day to see that your scar had disappeared." Guess what! His prophecy did come to fruition, as I have caught up with many colleagues today and even achieved as much as I have wanted in terms of significance, living a purposeful life, knowledge and more.

Take away: If you are at the crossroads as you read this memoir, thinking age is not on your side and that your circumstances are already making you feel you have not achieved much, I encourage you to stay hopeful. You should understand that we all are running different races; so, work at your pace and be focused. The tide will soon turn in your favour. Better days are here!

Life Lesson

5

THE GIFT OF RELATIONSHIP

iterally, can anyone walk through life alone? Obviously not! Why is this so? You will realise that individuals who do not make friends will at some point suddenly realise that holding hands with people can be somewhat important. In other words, we all need quality relationships to achieve bigger dreams and giant strides in life. Earlier on, I mentioned that I was an introvert for the most part of my formative years. But when I realised that being in the right environment puts me in a better position to attract purposeful individuals who would fast-track my journey, I had no option but to change. Examine yourself and see if you are rightfully positioned with the right set of people you need in your life per time.

Take away: When we talk about relationships, we cannot rule out the place of attraction and honour. Take out time to appreciate and honour those relationships God has brought your way. Honour them with some sort of gifts and appreciation, nurture them with kind words. Nothing is ever too small or expensive in this regard. Because what you don't honour/appreciate cannot confer benefits on you. We can only attract what we honour.

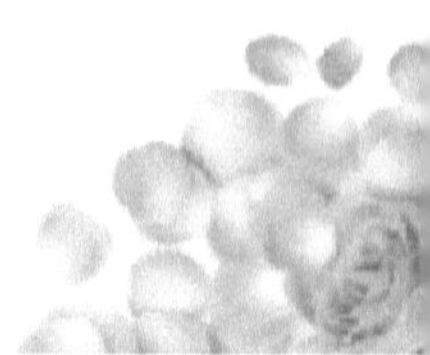

Life Lesson

6

GETTING RID OF TIMIDITY

I used to be very timid. I mean timidity in every sense of it. I could lock myself indoors for weeks. A lot of people saw nothing wrong and thought it was just fine for me to keep to myself. What they did not understand was my battle with timidity. I was afraid of not saying the right thing. I wanted people to validate me and when expectations were not met, I would withdraw into my shell. How did I escape this phase? I became more open and dealt with timidity by reading books that pointed me in the direction of self-worth and growth. I became self-aware and had a change of mindset, which made me see the need to approve myself before anyone else would. Gradually, I became very bold, though the process was not a walk in the park. Ever since, I have become better at relating with people and nurturing great relationships. This year has indeed ushered me into a new chapter and given me so much clarity. The word from God for me this year is "Year of Knowledge", this has made me realise the need to be in the right circle of influence and investment in personal development. Now, I can boldly say the best way to get rid of timidity is to act like it never exists. Just make a move and before you know it, you are absolutely achieving great feats.

Take away: Work on your emotion. If you need to engage an expert, the better for you. Share your fears and open up to someone who has positive influence over your life. However, master the art of compromise in your dealings. Absorb what's important in every conversation, and hangout with people who celebrate you.

Life Lesson

7

FACE YOUR FEARS

Have you ever seen a child who is crawling before? The child wants to explore standing and moving unaided. One would often wonder if there is inner energy which propels a child to face every hindrance in the way of achieving his/her goals. Fear is never an option even when the child falls several times, she/he still tries. However, that was not the case with me. I used to be very fearful as I constantly battled stage fright and was unable to communicate with people because I felt my knowledge of grammar was bad. This continued for a while until I made a career choice to study Mass Communication and that was the game changer for me. I became very vocal and could interact easily with peers and others alike.

Take away: A major shift for anyone, as it was for me, is finding your voice, finding your place and doing what gladdens your heart. Use your pain as a source of motivation for your journey.

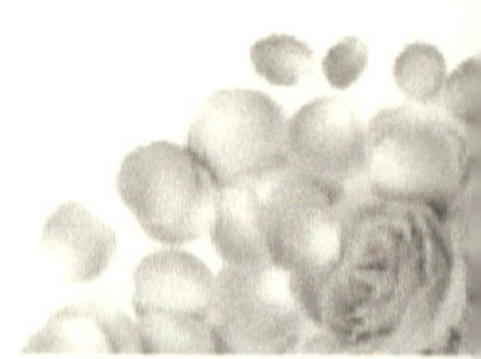

Life Lesson

8

SUPPORT SYSTEM

The need for a good support system on your journey through life cannot be over emphasized. I am most grateful to God for people I have met in my career, family, business, brethren in church and the like. I am grateful for the gift of my mother. She is such a perfect description of who a support system is. There was a time in my life I needed to navigate my career path. I got a job, but was not sure I could trust a nanny enough to look after my baby. I spoke with my mum and pleaded with my dad to release her for at least a year when I would wean my baby. Dad kindly obliged and having mum around was such a big relief for me. At the expiration of one year, she got me a great nanny, one I call "the best". Years after, I can boldly say I will employ that woman over and over again. That is what a good support system does for you. It makes your journey easy. We all need such people in our day-to-day life.

Take away: Having a support system is like a free flow of water from a fountain. If need be, outsource areas of your life that are more demanding. It only shows that you give priority to what's important, and this in return aids your sanity. You are not God, and you can't be everywhere.

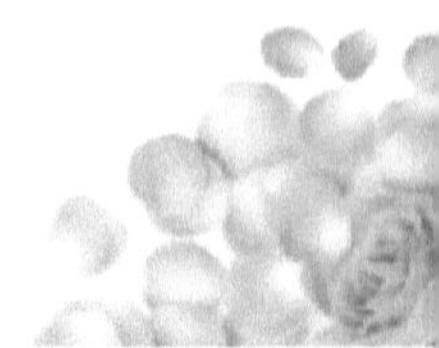

Life Lesson

9

VALUE-ADDED COMMUNITY

I really do not like to overburden people, so, naturally, I rarely ask for help. However, I have come to realise that if you really desire to achieve more, you may need to consider having a few circles of influence that could help to support, nurture and grow your purpose. One of the things I enjoy the most in this life journey is the community of individuals I constantly rub minds and shoulders with. I have become very vocal in my own circle and it is amazing how relevant I have become over the years.

Take away: I will encourage you to keep your circle small but ensure your voice is heard.

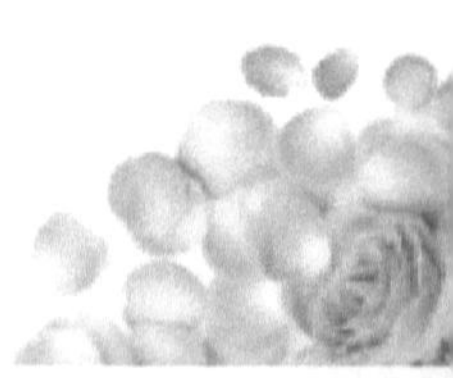

Life Lesson

10

LIFE IS A JOURNEY

It has been many years getting to this point in my life and I have come to see life as a journey which has given me the opportunity to evolve. Interestingly though, I was not like this. I remember some years back when I got a job and some of my colleagues felt I was undeserving of the particular position I was given. They could not understand why the management would consider the "extremely quiet " and "always moody" me for such position. They were not wrong about their reservations about me because what they pointed out were "demons" I was quietly dealing with. I was always moody and withdrawn and that made it difficult for me to be a great team player. My results on job deliveries were excellent, but my social interaction with colleagues was poor, to say the least. I was bitter about this for a while, but I knew that was not the solution to that challenge. So, I intentionally sought ways to get better at relating with people. I worked on my emotions and realised I had to create my own happiness. I also understood that embracing negativity had a way of holding me back. Today, I look back and I am grateful for the push I gave myself to become this new me everyone relates with easily now. My life has indeed been a journey and I am grateful for the criticisms that lead to my mind shift.

Take away: We are mortals, and the best of us is flawed. Let's constantly practice constructive criticism and not killing of the soul. Let's constantly support other people to succeed. We all need one another on this journey to self-discovery and actualization.

Life Lesson
11

THE LONELY PATH

We all go through the lonely path in our journeys. However, mine is different from yours. Most of us have something in our past or at the moment that seems like a powerful memory. It may be a traumatic event, heartbreak, betrayal, death of loved ones or the feeling of losing a dear one (like the death of Ibidunni Ighodalo). It could also be years of being at the receiving end of bullying, rape, rejection, abuse, ill-treatment, volatile temperament and whatnot. You know what? I have had my share too.

There was this season in my life, barely after my final examination in secondary school, the enemy struck. I was diagnosed with Venous leg ulcer - very devastating news I must say. For a young girl like me, with a beautiful future yet untapped, that news was heartrending. This actually led to several events which lasted for close to 2 years. At some point, I was walking with crutches due to several surgical operations on that particular leg. The last option was a skin grafting. Many thanks to everyone who stood by me in that season of my life. It was indeed a trying time for me.

God came through for me and healed me completely. Except you come really close to me, you will hardly know I have such a scar. There was something I learnt from that experience which I consider very important now. While I was in the hospital, I sat UTME and GCE and failed woefully. One thing is, I have always had this resilient attitude towards life; hence, the reason I did those two exams. My WASSCE result was withheld in 1997/1998

and my parent did not want to take chances. So, while on the hospital bed, they constantly encouraged me never to lose focus.

I guess a lot could have contributed to my failure, which made me think my mates had gone ahead of me. My WASSCE result was later released, but I failed English Language. I eventually got discharged from the hospital at a set time and thereafter gave my all to pursue my career. Though that phase of my life was such a lonely path for me, I am glad it did not make me give up on my dreams.

Take away: If it's that important to you, then, give it all the energy it requires. Age is only a number.

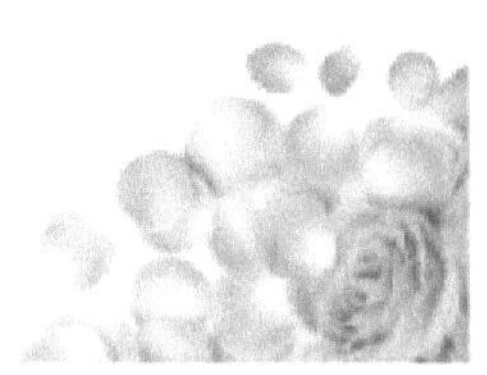

Life Lesson
12

IDEA RULES THE WORLD

At different times in my high school years, I had to change locations and usually looked forward to the holiday seasons when I would spend time with my family. The highpoint of the holidays was always the opportunity I had to go with mum to Lagos for Christmas shopping. Most times, I went with the list of items needed for resumption the following year. But this time round, I had a life-changing experience. While with her, I bought some fancy cups and other gift items which I knew would appeal to friends around me with some of my pocket money. Just as I predicted, I sold all and had to look for ways of keeping up with demands as they poured in. That was the beginning of business for me. Ever since, it has been a smooth sailing part of my life. I must say my uncle, Mr. Peter Oyeneye, also contributed immensely to building my interest in business.

Take away: Give attention to some little details of your life, do not ignore them. Attention is the first step in the learning process.

Life Lesson

13

EXPOSURE AND EXPERIENCE
ARE GREAT TEACHERS

At a point in my life, I lived with my uncle. Uncle Peter would wake me up and ask me to prepare to attend several presentations with him. This gave me lots of exposure. I can vividly remember some of the places I had been with him: Hill Station Hotel, Jos; Jerrotel, Jos; NICON Training School, Jos (where I met Chika Okpala, MFR, a Nigerian comedian popularly known as Chief Zebrudaya Okoroigwe Nwogbo alias 4:30, of the one time TV comedy series, New Masquerade); Plateau Hotel, Jos; Federal College of Forestry, Jos; Agura Hotel, Abuja; International Conference Centre, Abuja; NICON Hilton Abuja, UAC Training Centre, Apapa, Lagos and many more. I did not quite enjoy following him then. Little did I know I was being taught the art of selling and building self-confidence.

My uncle would organise award ceremonies with top government functionaries in attendance and would assign me roles. I really bless God for this man.

He also taught me the act of thinking, strategic selling and how best to generate selling ideas. He would say to me, "Remi, you may not know anyone. But I tell you, if you have the right dress sense and can communicate very well, coupled with a good disposition, you can sell to anyone at anytime." He would also say: "When you make an attempt, the response is either yes or no. But without any attempt, the answer is no. In the end, you are enriched by the experience" True to his words, I would not trade the experience I got from being exposed to such gatherings for anything as it did a lot to my psyche positively.

Take away: Embrace every opportunity to get exposed to new experiences. There is always a lesson money can't buy from such opportunities.

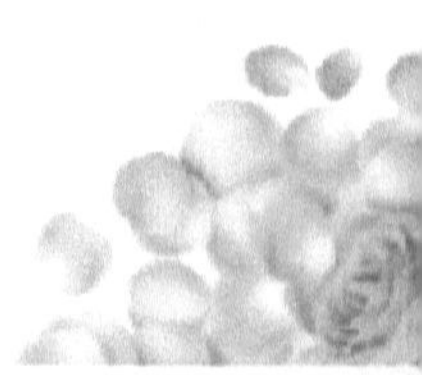

Life Lesson

14

WISDOM IS PROFITABLE TO DIRECT

My mantra has always been this: "If I get a 'no' today, I look forward to the next 'yes'". The truth is, even in your own pain, there will always be that point where you know you have found purpose. At some point in my life, God told me; "Remi, when a situation seems too overwhelming, allow Me and choose to respond rather than react."

Take away: To respond to life's troubles simply means to surrender our concerns to God and leave them there. That is wisdom! John McDonnell once said: "Every problem introduces a person to himself." This simply means that each time we encounter a painful experience, it affords us the opportunity of getting to know ourselves a little better.

Life Lesson
15

WHEN YOU ARE LOVED

I was in my teens when I left for Jos. There, I met beautiful people from different tribes and languages and we all became one big family. I remember how I used to be timid. Whenever I was asked to engage in activities in the church, I was always too shy to hold a microphone. Even though I was very good at some of these things, I was too conscious of making mistakes. The thought of wrong pronunciation or forgetting my lines and other "what-ifs" limited me in more ways than I could imagine. How I moved from "I can't do this" to "I can" was the power of association. I became very conscious of my circle of friends. Suddenly, I realised that people loved to be around me. I felt loved and I loved people in return. I became more drawn to individuals who were above my age. So, whenever I decided to pay someone a visit, the reception was always so exceptional such that I became very assertive of myself. Then, I discovered there was possibly an aura my personality exuded when I was around such individuals. I enjoyed the gathering of brethren even much more. It was during this period I found my love for village outreaches ignited by Dr. and Mrs. Francis Asieba, a lovely couple. I also joined a club called Daughters of Sarah, where we were taught about chastity. It was a whole lot of beautiful experiences to find genuine love amongst people. My experience in Jos was such a wholesome one that I cannot forget even in years to come.

Take away: Get along with like-minded people. Borrow encouragement from them! Be inspired by them!

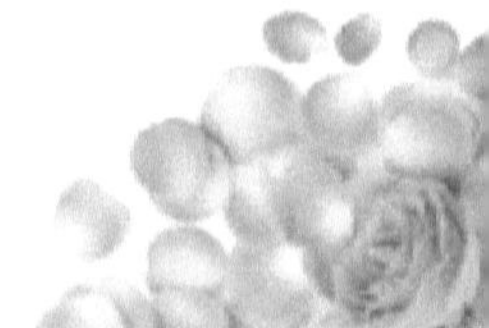

Life Lesson

16

SUPPORT FROM FRIENDS

The very first support I ever experienced can be traced to brethren from the Anglican Youth Fellowship I belonged then. Those were good old days of fellowshipping which made me look forward to our December retreats. The support from them, when I was hospitalised for close to 2 years, could not be quantified. Remembering the prayers for, letters written to and concern about me then brought back some emotions while writing this memoir. I must confess that I have enjoyed the company of good people and still do. My business growth can also be traced to the overwhelming love I get from people who often engage with my posts on my different social media platforms.

Take away: I am very big on support, and here is my advice to you: support your friends, listen to their ideas, share their posts, celebrate their victories and remind them of the role they play in your life. A little support from you can go a long way in someone's life.

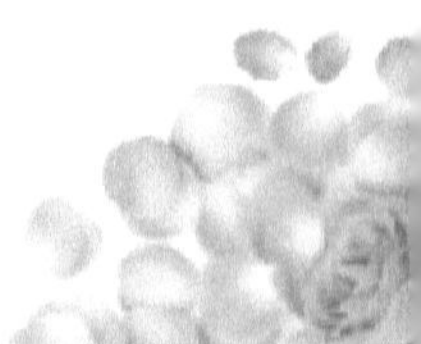

Life Lesson

17

ADD VALUE

I remember when I first read a book written by T. D. Jakes, The Lady, Her Lover and Her Lord. It is such an inspiring book. I set out early in life to be very resourceful. While trying to achieve this purpose, it dawned on me that I could be a very independent woman. Not necessarily because I did not need people's support but because I needed to pay attention to every aspect of my life and take ownership. I really wanted to become valuable to myself and to others, just like a woman on a mission. So, right from school days, I had always loved to help. I remember that growing up, each time I returned from school then, the first thing I did was to take off my school uniform, pick a broom and make straight for my parents' bedroom. I would sweep every corner, lay their bed, wash the bathroom and all I just wanted to achieve was to etch my presence in their heart. When I visit you, I am that girl that will take my plate to your kitchen to wash except you say otherwise.

This became a part of me even when I became a grown-up. I have always loved to support people and this in a way for me has greatly influenced what I do now. Today, I pride myself to say I help clients solve spontaneous needs. It has always been in me and whenever I find myself in the right community, I deliver excellently.

Take away: Like footprints in the sand, make people feel your presence in their lives. Let your imprints be felt. Make someone feel loved and secure because you are part of their life's journey. Be the reason why someone doesn't give up.

Life Lesson

18

TENDER BUT FIERCE

One fact about me is that I can be a very loyal friend until you show me the way of betrayal. When that happens, you have lost a friend in me without your knowledge. I just have a way of detaching myself from such people without any reservation. Oh, I can be very loyal to you. But please, do not betray my trust. I am a woman of few friends; however, I guard my relationship with friends jealously. As much as I do not easily make friends, I know that people are drawn to me. So, it takes me so much time to be committed to you. Yes, I know most people have countless individuals they enjoy spending time with and are involved with on a regular basis. But what is rare these days is the kind of friends who are involved in our lives. We must ask ourselves what exactly is the quality of such friendship. As a result of some not-too-pleasant experiences I have had with people, I am always careful to allow time prove if a friend is really worth trusting.

Take away: Identify with people whose purpose align with yours. Not everyone will fit into your vision, so keep your circle small and learn by observation.

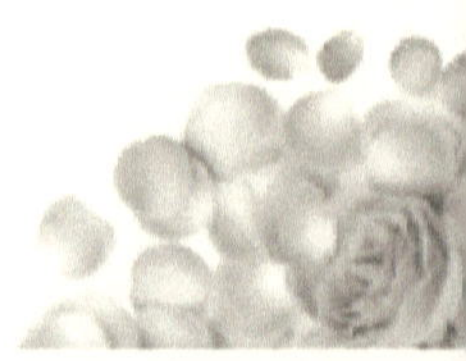

Life Lesson
19

THE YOUNGER GENERATION

In April 2013, I started a movement called "Dream Reality Africa". This desire was born out of my passion for the younger generation. It used to be a monthly gathering where I invited few friends within my circle to support with their knowledge and expertise, using that channel to impact the lives of these young ones. The funding was completely on me. I used to move from one school to another, enlightening young ones on the need to embrace "doing business on the side" alongside their careers. I always preached the gospel of future relevance and the need to be well positioned in their chosen careers. Through the platform, we were able to produce individuals who are doing excellently with different skills which have built them steady flow of passive income besides what their main career offers them.

Take away: Life is not certain, but opportunities are immense. Lots of services will be needed in this present time (The new Normal). Even though some are losing their jobs, other people are picking new jobs because they have developed new competencies and skills. Only those who can solve specific problems will become relevant. So, no one should say they aren't cut out for some skills. We must position ourselves to learn new skills and equip ourselves, especially digitally.

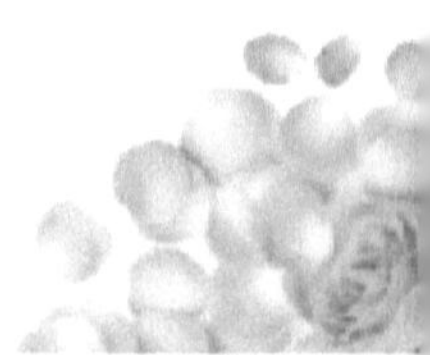

Life Lesson

20

PAYING AND ACCEPTING COMPLIMENTS GRACEFULLY

I naturally find myself attracted to people who show kindness and pay compliments and I am sure a lot of people feel the same way. I have a coach whose speaking engagements have become my tonic. Often after her session, she would ask me how it went. Asking for my feedback has become something she looks forward to, not necessarily to validate her but to encourage her. Just like my coach, everyone needs encouragement at one point or the other in life. It is only natural that they expect to get it from fellow humans. So, for me, I have learnt to show kindness to people and pay them great compliments because I understand how well they make them feel. It is then safe to say that as much as you love to be complimented, never fail to pay others compliments too. It makes the world go round.

Take away: This sums it up.

Normalize complimenting good things in yourself or in others. Train your mind to acknowledge beautiful things in others. Strengthen your commendation muscles. Lavish genuine affirmation on whoever deserves it. Criticize less.
It's a hack for draining the power of envy and jealousy.
(Sola Adesakin, 2020)

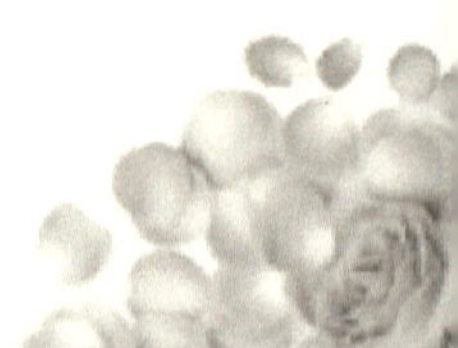

Life Lesson 21

MORE THAN ENOUGH

"Every woman who desires to walk with God goes through all shades of storms, winds and rain. Her life is filled with challenges and victories. She is like the anointing oil that was mixed by the apothecary. She is a careful blend of life's many spices. Her personality is a pot pourri of different things which years of knowing her will not disclose all that makes her who she is.

According to T. D. Jades (2000) in his book, The Lady, Her Lover and Her Lord:

> **She is carefully accosted and shortly simmered, stirred patiently by her Lord. It is amazing how patient God is preparing her for destiny. He knows how long it takes. He knows what events it will take to bring her to a place of maturity in Him. He is emphatically her Lord.**

I read the above many years back and the words in earnest capture my thoughts in this lesson of my life's journey. Indeed, God has been gracious to me because while I may not have the best of everything I desire yet, He has been at the centre of it all. He is bringing me into my wealthy place. Hallelujah! I therefore make bold to say that God is more than enough for me.

Take away: As the seasons of weather change, so do our lives and God's dealings with us. However, the first step is to identify and understand the season you are in. Spring is characterised by fruitfulness, newness, the inception of life, blooming and freshness. Summer is marked by the production of harvest, and

the activity of the hustle and bustle of life. In fall, we see the signs of change, the coolness of the winds and bright vibrant colours. Winter is marked by stillness, quietness, whereby no signs of life can be seen. These seasons come and go in their time. Through every season, there is an assignment.

Life Lesson

22

IMPACTING LIFE

What really counts most about our success in life is measured by the lives of individuals we are able to impact. I am certain it is never in the volume of wealth we are able to acquire. When I started out my online business fully in 2016, I was more particular about the number of people I would impact. I wanted to replicate my drive and energy in as many people I could. In my quest for discovering how best to go about this, I discovered a lot of ladies loved the idea of doing side businesses but their income would not allow them. So, what did I do? I decided to bridge this gap by acting as an intermediary/middle woman in helping to deliver their requested goods to them while they in return would sell to people without necessarily affecting their present jobs. When I started, I had just one client I was outsourcing for and I did it so well until she got a new job in another state. However, all efforts to persuade her to continue proved abortive as she could not keep up with the demands of the new environment and the ripple effect on her side business. In a way, beyond words, I know God used me to impact her greatly. I cannot begin to mention individuals I have been able to mentor when it comes to starting their own side business and many consultations I have had to do with individuals who have started their own businesses today. I can only appreciate God for using me as a channel and nothing more. Recently, as part of my own little way to impact people's lives, I started a WhatsApp group called MSS (Mind Shift Series), which is now registered and has become a

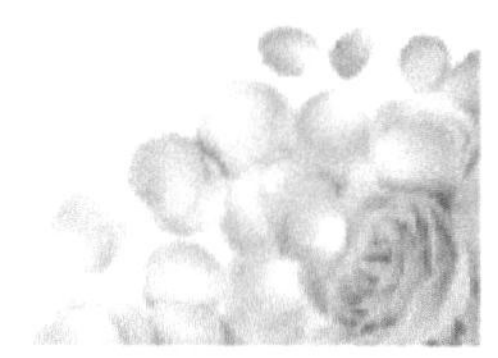

full-fledged online school called Mind Shift Series Academy (MSSA), with quite a good number of people on the platform. The feedback I got via direct messages and phone calls months to its official launch were mind-blowing. The platform is available and is free for only those who are ready to take their entrepreneurship journey a step higher.

Take away: A life of impact is the most important. There are people who have died and cannot be forgotten for a long time, and there are also others who are still alive and cannot be remembered. What makes the difference between the two is impact! Until we live to give, we are not alive at all. Live every day with a sense of purpose and urgency.

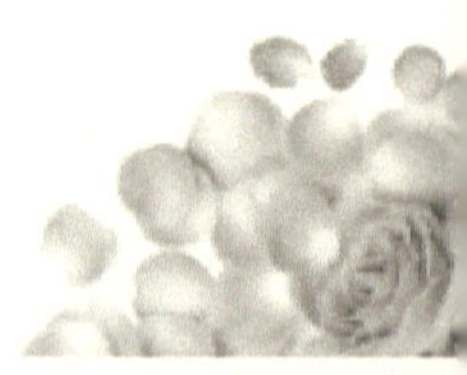

Life Lesson 23

MIND SHIFT

Mind shift can be achieved if only you have discovered the essence of your being. The ability to connect your dotted lines becomes very important as you gravitate towards a mind shift process. It all starts from the mind. In view of my experience and exposure, I become burdened that many people can make significant progress, just as I have done in business and career by the grace of God. Sadly, this has not been the case for some individuals. I was pressed and persuaded that some people can be helped to achieve more, and this can be made possible through the support from a value added community of others. Mind Shift Series Academy was put together to rub minds with like-minded people, share experiences, failures and successes and see the possible ways of moving from one level to the other through a learning process.

Take away: In other words break through obstacles. You must come out of the old to walk in the new. Give much time to learning and discover your hidden potential. It is important for our mind to shift because our thought pattern informs our actions. Everything happens first in the mind. If you'll pay a little more attention, you will see this. Get on board to becoming what you're destined to be.

Life Lesson 24

CALLING THEM FORTH

As much as I love to operate from the background, I have come to understand that the times we are in requires correct and effective positioning and projection of our brand. To do this, we must be seen and heard. It is indeed obvious that the global space has got so much to offer everyone who would love to be seen and heard. The pandemic which brought about a new normal further exposes us to the possibilities that exist on the online space. Everyone is compelled to embrace the new normal or be phased out of the scheme of things. So, you may be asking: "How do I go about this?" You should understand that this is the era of building a community of like-minds - calling forth the kind of people you want into your space. I knew what I wanted when I started out in business. My aim has always been and still is to be of service to First Ladies of States and individuals in authority. That is a goal which has not changed.

Take away: Identify your circle and when you do, don't play small. Be intentional.

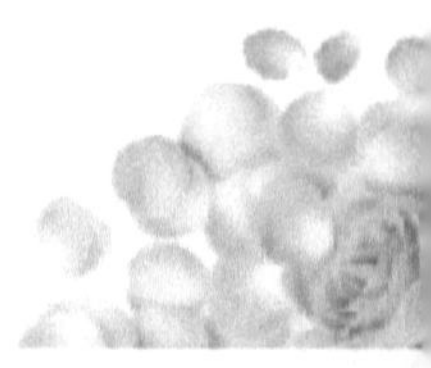

Life Lesson

25

HOLD YOUR PARENTS DEAR

One of the best gifts God gave everyone is the gift of parents. Our parents play a major role in our individual lives. When we appreciate and honour our parents, we please God. After all, it was God's idea. In Ephesians 6:1-3, Paul admonished us, saying:

Children, obey your parents, for this is right. Honour your father and mother - which is the first commandment with a promise that it may do well with you and that you may enjoy long life on earth.

I stress this subject because not only is it a commandment but also one of the criteria for longevity. What happens to individuals who do not get close to their parents? How about those whose memories of their parents are not so dear? How do you respond when the legacy you are left with is embarrassing, traumatic or too tainted by pain to remember any good? If you are having trouble honoring your parents, then you may need to get down to the root of the matter and check what is wrong. You sure need to realise that a parent's love is more important to a child than wealth, education or any form of material possession. I implore you to hold your parents dear. They are a major determinant of your success in life. If they are no more, you should hold the people who stand in that gap as parents for you in great honour and esteem.

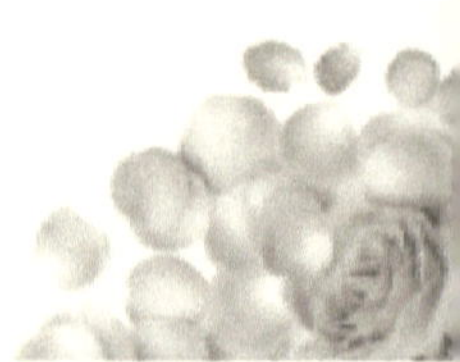

Take away: It is important to consciously plan to reward and take care of whoever God has placed over your life as an authority. Ensure you roll out your plan as soon as possible. It is a matter of urgency. Suggested treats for parents and others in their position may include a photo session, a trip, fruits basket, vouchers, movie, shopping experience, variety of tea/beverages, medical attention and many more. We must not underestimate the power God bestows on these people.

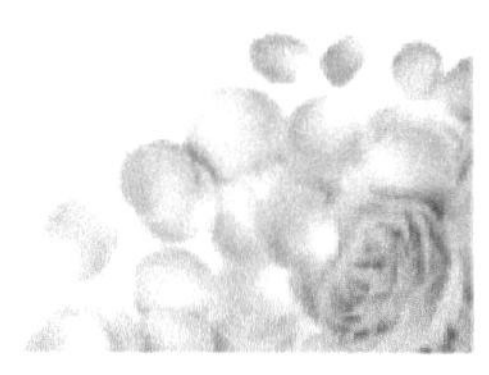

Life Lesson
26

MY YOUNGER SISTER

My younger sister is an embodiment of care and love. We share a close bond and it will be difficult for anyone to know that I am 10 years older than she is. This lady is someone you can call your right-hand man. She has always been there. She is one kind of creature anyone would love to have as a sibling. She has my back always. I remember the time she paid me a visit when I was heavily pregnant. She broke down in tears as soon as she arrived

My pregnancy was really overwhelming for her. I was craving for moin-moin just as she arrived. Typical of her lovely self, she swung into action. Sadly, by the time she was done cooking, pregnancy craving changed; moin-moin did not appeal to me anymore. My action moved her to tears as it dawned on her that her effort to satisfy me had been put to waste. When she got over her emotion, she explained to me how she had wanted to satisfy my craving but for the swing of mood fueled by my pregnancy. It was such an emotional moment for both of us. Toluwalope, you have been such a bundle of joy. I am so grateful to God for the gift of you, my darling sister. You have had your own share of life and its attendant struggles, but you have not allowed any of them to deter you. Rather, you are beautiful and strong in your own way, darling sister. Thank you for sharing your life with me. Dee, Tamilore, Tirenioluwa and I are grateful for all you have done for us. I love you!

Take away: Write a short note to your siblings (delete - sister/siblings) post it on their wall or send to them as an email. It can be thrilling!

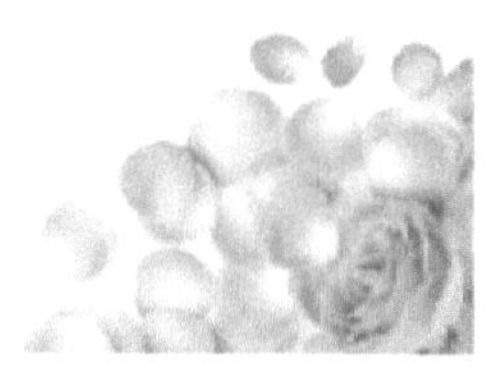

Life Lesson

27

MY FAMILY

I was raised by very strict parents and how I managed to go through life with them remains a wonder. However, growing up has made me realise my parents imposed stringent rules on me and I could not even think of negotiating majority of them.

A few questions come to mind now. Was the social environment for the children better then than what we have today? Well, in some ways, I will say yes. Why? This is because our parents trusted us enough to go out and play with friends unsupervised. We could travel long distances with our cousins without our parents getting worried. I remember a time I travelled with some of my cousins to Ibadan and the only adult with us on that journey was the driver. Despite enjoying this much freedom, our parents never failed to instill in us morals of a lifetime. We were taught to draw the line between freedom and waywardness. Today, I am still enjoying those lessons.

It is quite sad to note that things are no longer like that these days. Morality seems to have become a thing of the past. What we had to watch on television then was a far cry from what our children get to watch today. The focus is more on entertainment now, while education is taking the back stage. Growing up, I used to participate in a lot of social activities, cultural dance (bolojo), stage plays, fashion parades (my costumes were usually top notch), nature's corner (this is where we would bring different food items for display at one corner in the classroom), etc. I used to be at my best at anything fashion; you know when you are asked to dress all by yourself in a competition - and I was usually the first to finish dressing up. These were some of the activities that helped us to be independent, take decisions and be responsible. Even though as I grew older, some of the skills started waning for reasons I could not tell. Did I also mention that I used to be the best dressed in school and some social activities? These, for me, were my childhood competencies. They actually say a lot about us and the things that were so dear to us. Little wonder, I love anything aesthetics. I love beauty. I had and still have a picture of the apartment I wanted then in my head to date. There is just a way some of these competencies play out in our lives as individuals. I also love the music of my younger years. Oh my days!

I used to be very outgoing and popular during my childhood days. Who did not know Remi? I was always involved in party dancing competitions and all. I could sing lyrics of choice songs. Perhaps that is why it is not a surprise that I love singing. I was a very active member of my church choir. All of those social competencies were diverted into church activities and I can really say, I played my roles well. Speaking of music, I loved music when I was much younger. I enjoyed my music lessons a great deal during my secondary school days. I remember Mr. Tunde Ladipo was my music teacher then. My dad loved to play the music of the legendary Orlando Owoh, Ebenezer Obey, King Sunny Ade and the like. Simi Gold, nee Ogunleye and some other folks seem to be getting the good old vibes these days though. I also love the old movies. I personally think they are pretty good. Although it was only outside my house I could watch secular movies because my parents won't permit us to watch any movies apart from Mount Zion's movies in my house. However, there are a lot of recent movies that I know are pretty good, especially Tyler Perry's series and a lot of Nigerian movies. With Netflix, I can say that the world has evolved and is still evolving.

Print journalism was more popular then and you would see many people reading newspapers. Today, broadcast journalism and social media have taken over, reducing the power and influence of print media. In all, my childhood experiences are my major competencies, which I have developed over time. Today, they actually play a crucial role in my journey to the big 40. But like we always say: "Adulthood is a scam."

Take away: Our family values are a reflection of who we are. If the values are good, and if we articulate and live them, they will help shape the next generation positively. The next generation will therefore be better as they will be able to express themselves better, solve problems effectively, grow and learn faster.

Life Lesson

28

THE POWER OF DREAMS AND REVELATION

dream a lot and I have a personal relationship with God who is my Father. I love it more when my dreams materialise whether for me or someone else. I was not so particular about dreams until March 2018. I was part of a 21-day father-daughter challenge organised by Omilola Oshikoya. Oh, what an experience! I had the privilege of writing a letter to God during the challenge and my relationship with Him grew bigger. I did see God in a deeper light. On Day 1, the organiser asked us who God was to us. I responded by saying that "He's an expression of faithfulness." In many ways, God has proven to me to be the ever-present God. In my darkest moments, He was there for me. He is my healer. He is my Ebenezer. He gives me ideas to run with. He helps me through my career path. Indeed, I have been marvelously helped by God. Here is one of the letters I wrote to God:

Dear Father,

I love You dearly. I have missed You so much, especially in songs and personal discussion. I am coming back to the place of worship out of my love for You. No one could love me the way You do. You have embraced me and I love You in return. This is a love letter to You, written to let you know that You are still in my heart. I still carry You around in my heart. Though the challenges of life have taken me far away.

Little did I know what You had in store for me when You told me this year was my year of "devotion". I have always loved You even though I may not show it. Whenever I go my way, You always have a way of bringing me back to you. I am in love with you because when no one feels my pain in this race, You do and You are constantly challenging me to take up this assignment as one of my purposes in life, even though the process for me is very tough.

Today, I return to You. I have come to accept and resolve in my mind that there was a reason why You gave me all that's within me. I resolve to be thankful and say yes to Your will.

Thank You for this healing process and for where you are leadingme this 2018, my Year of Devotion.

Yours simply devoted to You,

Remilekun Kehinde-Philip

The above was the letter I wrote to God in 2018 during the father-daughter 21-day challenge. One of the major reasons I do not give up on myself and people is basically because of my love for God. I have experienced too much of God such that I do not easily give up on people, most especially those who are close to me. Shortly after this encounter, I became very serious with my dreams and revelation. Thanks to all who have helped me to navigate this process. A lot of times, I do not even understand some of those dreams. But then, God placed individuals around me that helped in analysing them per time. Some are yet to come true, while some have. I still trust God so much in this aspect of my life, for clarity and purpose. Selah!

Take away: Nurture your gift/giftings. Constantly work on sharpening your talents. Be sensitive about God's dealings in your life. Every gift that you have received comes with a measure, because man is mortal. God won't give you more than you can contain. However, your gift has a way of replicating itself into branches. So, spread your wings and fly.

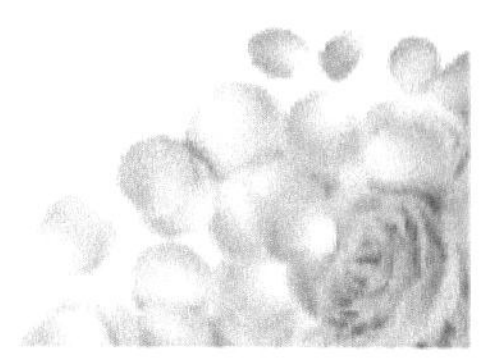

Life Lesson

29

MY CHILDREN

My children are such a delight. Have you ever heard me talk about them before? I speak about them with a lot of passion. I had a lot of challenges during conception. That I went through that process and survived the journey is a confirmation that I can cross every hurdle and pain. It was a journey of faith. I was between life and death. At some point when I could not bear the process, I would tell the doctor to evacuate the baby as everything around me came to a standstill.

From the second week of conception, living would become a challenge for me and the miracle baby in my womb. My family, friends and neighbours could not understand how pregnancy could bring so much pain. But the moment I brought forth, you would hardly believe it was me. My energy and strength would be restored, as evidenced by my voice. This is the same person who could not pick calls, but i would now be very joyful and vocal. That was a process no one but the Giver of miracles could understand. God is great.

I remember my days as a paid employee. When I resumed work after delivery, I would narrate my pregnancy experience with so much joy. Some miracles are birthed when we go through life's journey. Only you can feel the pain. Sometimes, you cannot explain the pain you feel on the inside. But when that particular phase is over, everyone rejoices with you and calls you different beautiful names. That is the joy these children bring to me. Watching them grow in grace and doing things which make God happy are the totality of my being. You are loved and appreciated, my dear children. Men and women will call you both blessed.

Take away: Take few minutes to pray for your child/children, children born or yet unborn. Every prayer is a seed.

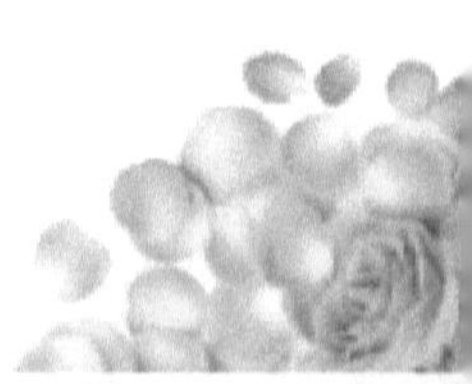

Life Lesson
30

MY PARTNER

Funny enough, I don't know how I got to put this on lesson 30. As far as I know, we got married the year I was going to clock 30. You desire to take me to the Bahamas, it's a matter of time, it will happen. Tamilore and Tirenioluwa loves the way you father them, and they desire you do more. Its 10 years of doing life together, and in spite of it all, God has indeed been gracious to us. Thank you for helping me discover myself. Your input in all I do, makes the difference. You keep telling me, I am not romantic, lol. My number one fan and cheerleader. There can be no Remilekun without Damilare. Perhaps one of the benefits of getting married to my husband is my desire to become a great force. Thank you for making me become one. It is actually deeper than what I can express in words. You are different from me in every way. But then, you have your own strength. I trust God that you will become everything God has designed you to be. Do not relent. Only become so much more; make God proud of your existence. My uttermost desire for you is in Proverbs 31. You are loved and appreciated.

Take away: Everyone has a dream. The totality of you is all wrapped together. You must discover yourself first and know who you are.

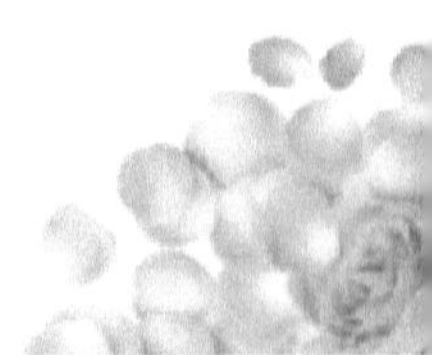

Life Lesson
31

CHILDHOOD EXPERIENCES

Recently, I called my parents to ask them about my childhood experiences. I wanted to find out those qualities peculiar to me while growing up. Dad began by reminding me how much of a party freak I was as a child. He told me I enjoyed attending birthday parties the most and on one of those occasions, my lovely black bag was stolen. Remembering that conversation while writing got me laughing seriously.

Dad also mentioned that I was such an independent child who could easily travel with anyone as long as there was food. I found this quite hilarious though because I am no longer a food person, although I always love to have enough snacks in the house. I remember him telling me how I was such a social child who participated actively in school competitions (cultural or academic).

Mum also told me how friendly I was as a child and that attracted the love of everyone around me. I almost could not believe that because as much as I love to make friends now, I hardly make the first move in friendship. She also spoke highly of my extreme neatness as a child. Looking back, I am grateful for how far I have come.

There is no doubt I have shed some of these characteristics, but I am still that lovely and accommodating Remilekun. My charisma has helped my business and relationship goals in no small measure.

Take away: There is only one you. So, be the best version of you, you can be as possible. You are an original, there are distinguishing factors that make you to be you. No one else can be who you are or do what you do. You are exceptional!

Life Lesson
32

THEY ALL MATTER - THE JOY AND THE PAIN

Life is indeed a journey. In Genesis 12:1-2, the Lord said to Abram (who was later renamed Abraham): **"Go from your country, your people and your father's household to the land I will show you. I will make you into a nation and I will bless you; I will make your name great, and you will be a blessing."**

Abraham did not know what his journey would look like before embarking on it. If he had had it all figured out, he would have protested or tried to make everything fall in place. But as we all know, God's ways are not known.

Abraham took his journey with absolute trust in the promises of God. At first, everything seemed okay until after a while, famine broke out. He embraced the process of surviving all the hurdles in his way and indeed made God proud.

Shortly after his encounter in Egypt, Abraham moved to Negev and the Lord kept his covenant with him still. It was recorded that he became very wealthy in livestock and in silver and gold when he was there. Remember, something was very constant in every phase God took Abraham through: his commitment to building an altar (communication with God). That was to ensure he was still in line with the scriptwriter; he was at the center of God's will. Then, there was another pain coming right from his very own family member, Lot. The Bible says, "When the way of a man pleases the Lord, even his own enemy will be at peace with him." Such was the case of Abraham when Lot decided to part with the juicy part of the land.

Do you think someone has cheated you? Have you been asking God if that was the plan written in the scripts for your life? Yes, it is! God is all-knowing, so, whatever it is you may be going through, He is in the picture. Can you see what God did? He made the covenant He had with Abraham again and said, "Look around from where you are, to the north and south, the east and west, they are all yours." Genesis 13:1 says, "All the land you see, I will give to you and your offspring forever."

Now, can you see all that played out with Lot in the 14th chapter? That is exactly what God takes away from you when you do not allow the pain of betrayal from friends, business and family to overwhelm you. You do not have to be petty over any situation; you only need to have a large heart and accommodate all that will be thrown at you. Did you also see Abraham's reaction when he heard that Lot had been taken captive? He called out the 318 trained men born in his household to rescue him." What a heart!

What we seem not to understand when we allow God is that, He will always come through with a better plan. In the process of helping his brother, he met King Melchizedek, who also re-affirmed God's promises over his life. In Genesis 14:19, King Melchizedek blessed Abraham, saying: "Blessed be Abram of

the God most high, possessor of heaven and earth". Then in chapter 15:1, God revealed Himself again to Abraham to re-affirm his covenant with him. Can you see the process? Do you know that feeling of belonging, when you are going through a difficult phase and God calls you by your name and speaks to you? Abba! It is a good feeling, I must confess!

God said to Abraham: "Do not be afraid, Abram. I am your shield, your very great reward." Of course, God knew his state of mind. He knew he had no heir yet, so he had to re-affirm him first. There are those times we feel all alone when we are going through some unpleasant phases despite seeing all God is doing through us. We often come to a state of emptiness and begin to ask God so many questions. The truth is, God indeed feels our pain. He knows when we ask him questions not from the place of fear but from the place of good intentions or from the place of selfishness but from where we feel it the most. Do you really feel God is far? No, He is not.

You remember the story of my leg I shared in Chapter 4? I have felt all alone before. I had to ask God questions, especially after the first skin grafting was done and I was still on the hospital bed for 30 days without moving. Though it was a challenging period of my life, God trusted me enough to manage the process and come out victorious. The Bible says, "For our present affliction or troubles are achieving for us an eternal glory that far outweighs them all." God told Abraham, "This man will not be your heir, but a son who is your own flesh and blood will be your heir." What a reassurance! Let God be true and every man be a liar. Has he said it? He will do it. Faithful is HE that has promised.

It happened that a day came in Abraham's journey that the promise was fulfilled. You and I are part of that promise God gave him. That was the joy that crowned it all. So, I will encourage you to wait on God. You are next in line for a miracle. Peace!

Take away: keep hope alive. Hope is the confident expectation that what we desire will become reality someday. It is trusting that everything will work out in the end. Speak positive and encouraging words over yourself each day. I became more deliberate about positive affirmation in recent times, and it works. Set goals, and speak life to those goals by speaking faith-filled words that will bring those goals to pass.

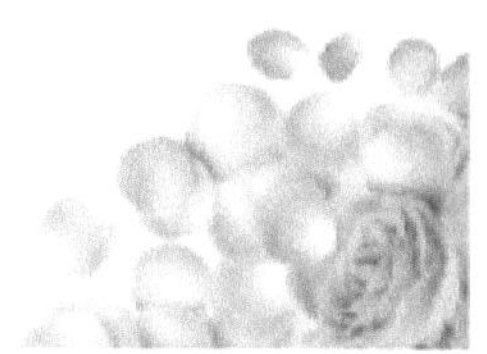

Life Lesson

33

MY COLLEAGUES

This memoir will be incomplete if I fail to talk about several wonderful colleagues I have met in the journey of life. I have worked with amazing individuals and I will plead that you allow me take you through my career journey. I started my career as a front desk manager. I was not friendly then and that put me in the bad book of my former colleagues. Although I had given my life to Christ then, I did not think there was anything wrong with my cold attitude in the workplace. I felt the office was meant for serious work and not making unnecessary acquaintances. I had no idea that was such a terrible mindset to have. That attitude denied me of so many opportunities in the workplace. This continued until a lady, who happened to be quite cordial with me, spoke about me to my boss and the outcome of their discussion got me enrolled in a finishing school.

Poise Nigeria was such an experience for me. While working there, I was able to gain mastery as to how to behave in the workplace, build relationship with colleagues and work ethics as regards managing visitors at the front desk. Why wasn't I doing it right in the first place? I was having relationship issues then. Rather than drop my troubles at home, I carried them with me to work every day and that affected my relationship with clients. Now, you need to understand that not too many people are lucky to have individuals who are ready to help them work on their emotions. I was just one of those lucky ones who happened to work with amazing personalities. So, I want to use this medium to say a big thank you to Florence for her help in my growth process. She is such a darling. She is someone everyone needs to have in their corner. I remember when I gave birth to my first child, she asked Toyin Mulero(nee Ajagunna), a former colleague to make pepper soup and deliver it to me at the hospital. What a genuine love from a colleague turned sister! Florence, I love you and you know it.

In the same vein, how can I ever forget the likes of Emmanuel Udoro, with whom I did quite a number of things and Yetunde Falade, Mummy Pinkie as we fondly call her. This woman is such a blessing. I have not seen any of my services which Yetunde Falade has not been a part of, whether directly or indirectly. I am so indebted to you. Everywhere I have worked left me with the gift of beautiful souls. Even the not-so-good ones still turned out to be good afterwards.

I fondly remember Ophylia Ibekwe as well. She is such a beautiful soul. I cannot forget Omotoke Idowu, my darling. I knew you as an intern years ago. But with each new day, I thank God for the great woman you have become. A big hug for Bolaji Abimbola of Indigo, whose act of kindness to me during my pregnancy days can never be forgotten. He would pick me to work every morning and was never tired of doing so till I had my child. Indeed, I have met beautiful people in life. When I wanted to quit my job and told Toke about it, she kept persuading me not to because she was not too convinced my Plan B would work. But today, without any iota of doubt, Toke is really fond of

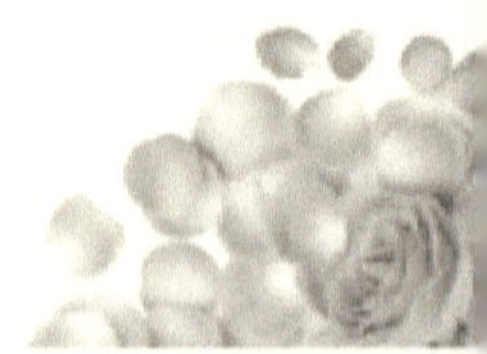

my passion. According to her, she wished she supported me early enough when I first had the conversation with her.

How can I forget Olajumoke Rufus? Toke Dawodu (nee Idowu) and Jumoke would ensure I bought the best wigs then. These ladies were sweet. I also remember Bolanle Atansuyi, my buddy during BD Consult days. Then I met another Bola who is one beautiful soul as well. To be honest, I really think it is okay to appreciate people in their lifetime; not when they are no more. Thank you to my LBS buddies at School of Media and Communication class of 2011. That was the year I was heavily pregnant with my first baby. I could not talk much or participate in class. Little wonder my son is a genius. This is a boy who attended an advanced school while in the womb.

In-between all of these beautiful memories, I have also experienced not so pleasant ones - office politics and the like but God be praised for all of our experiences in the journey of life. They all sum up who we really are today.

To God alone be all the glory.

Take away: Surround yourself with positive people. Be sure to guard your eyes, ears and mouth by surrounding yourself with positive people. This is called social wealth, we all need these set of individuals as we journey through life. Be sure to have people who are willing to share in and celebrate your successes.

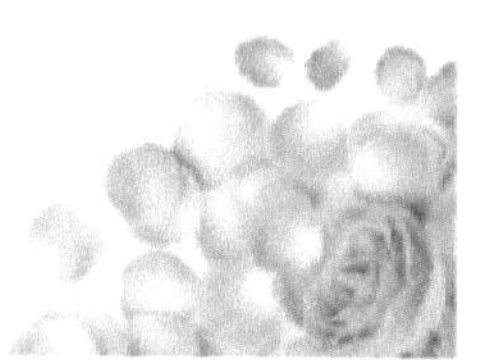

Life Lesson 34

MY LOVE FOR WHITE

My mum made me love white. As far I could remember, prior to my 5th birthday, my mum had always bought me a set of white socks and underwear. She taught me how to wash them well also. I remember how she would ask me to separate all white clothing and wash them in a separate bowl. I have since mastered the process of handling anything white. As young as I was then, I could clean my white canvass very well. It is no wonder people always admired me in school. You would never see my white socks look dirty in school. I know some of my schoolmates reading this will remember Remi and her sparkling socks. I could play in school, but my uniform and socks would still be very clean. Those features were my signature then and they still are.

This has gone on to translate into my love for anything white. I remember when I was selecting theme colours for my 40th birthday, I included a white dress and a pair of white shoes to match. I give credit to Mrs. Bidemi Onayinka who, upon receiving my order to have her make me a white dress, told me not to bother with the cost as she would love to gift me one. She runs a big fashion store and does training. If you like my dress, please do not hesitate to check her out.

Take away: Be sure to take practical steps to take care of yourself. Pamper yourself and practice self-care more often. Eat healthy food, fruits and vegetables, get plenty of rest and exercise. Set aside special time to treat yourself to something you enjoy, such as movie, dinner, pedicure or manicure. Be good to yourself, you sure deserve it.

Life Lesson
35

MY LOVE FOR GIFTS

My parents are loving people. My parents understood what it means to celebrate birthdays. If my memory serves me right, there was hardly a birthday we missed celebrating in my house. My love for gifts grew when I was preparing to go to the boarding school for my secondary school education. I was gifted a leather box I had secretly admired. It was one of those items dad bought on his numerous trips to Saudi Arabia. When it was time to label my items, I watched in admiration as dad scribbled my name on each of them. He did the arrangement in such a way that each item looked like a gift pack. Dad is one man I know who is meticulous with arranging things. So, all my years in the boarding school, I admired my own belongings so much that it built in me the love for gifts.

Other peculiar features about my parents, which made me a gift lover, are their love for celebrating birthdays and their disposition to how they treat visitors. It was a duty in our house to celebrate every child's birthday however little. The ceremony usually came with a beautifully wrapped gift of an item and cash for the celebrant. They were also big on making every visitor leave our house with a gift of some sort.

So, without mincing words, I took these lovely traits from my parents. It is one of the reasons I can excel effortlessly at the drop-shipping business I run now.

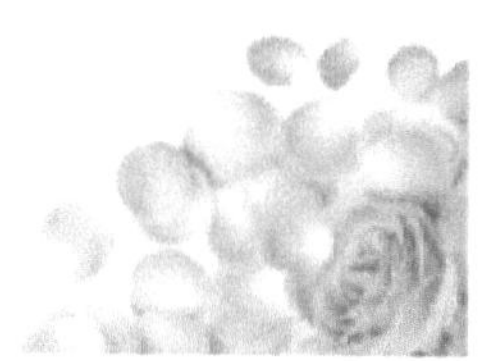

"It's not how much we give, but how much love we put into giving." -Mother Teresa

Take away: Giving a thoughtful gift takes just that thought! Offering to cook for someone who is hospitalized, volunteering on a friend's project, babysitting for a working mom, and helping as a support system for a friend with some health challenge can make all the difference.

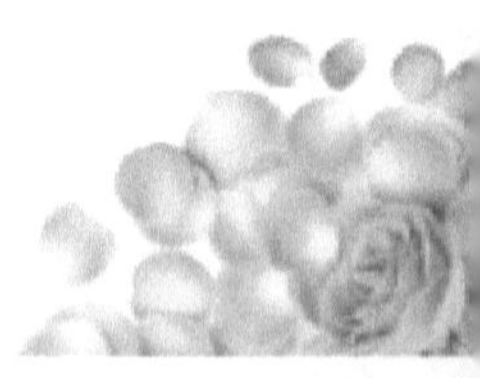

Life Lesson
36

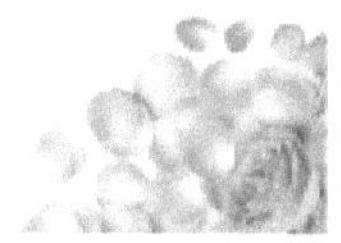

KAYP (KEHINDE-PHILIP)

started KAYP in July 2016. It was born out of passion and was a Plan B for my exit from paid employment. I had mentioned my plan to a colleague who had gone on to voice her fears for me. She was worried if it could sustain my family. Funnily enough, it was about the time my husband lost his job. So, I could understand her concern. Typical of me, I do not spend time over-analysing ideas as I usually think that could make me lose steam and miss the execution. I just believe that it is in the acting that you get things right. When you do not start it, you will not be able to know its possibility of success. I summoned the courage to resign. I must say it was indeed a step of faith. I am bold to say this now, as it was not looking like it as of that time.

When I began this journey, it was a lonely one for me. Thanks to mum who was always ready to help at any given time. That was how KAYP FOODS started. First of all, I created a WhatsApp group and added all my friends, big sisters, older family members and church members. I started and it was looking so promising. Because it was a transition for me, people believed and started placing orders.

Coincidentally, upon resigning my job, I was added to my secondary school alumni platform on WhatsApp. After introducing myself, I was given a role to teach on business every week. This I did diligently as time allowed me. Unknown to me, a senior from another set, late Olaide Akinode (may her soul rest in peace), who was mistakenly added to the group, took keen interest in what I was doing and wanted to replicate same in her own group – the Exceptional Women's Platform. Initially, when she reached out to me, I tried to decline the offer because I did not know how conveniently managing two platforms would be for me, given that I had a business to manage too. Nonetheless, I took the challenge and delivered excellently. That also increased the visibility for my business.

At a point, I had to return to school for a higher degree and that hampered my commitment. This made her create another group where we had more people who could take turns at facilitating the sessions. This brought about some relief for me especially. Interestingly, I began to replicate most of what I taught in my business too and the result was nothing short of excellence.

After a while, the alumni planned to hold the yearly reunion and I was delegated to cater for about 150 guests. What earned me that? My consistency and diligence of course! I initially wanted to decline the offer because KAYP was basically about the supply of raw food items and not full catering but later accepted it as a challenge. With the help of some ladies in the group, we delivered excellently.

Then, another transition happened in 2017 after I discovered a multi-level marketing food supply chain had emerged and was taking my customers from me, as some of them now preferred them. So, I prayed and told God I needed another source of income while I still had KAYP FOODS running by the side. God heard me. Meanwhile, I had been selling fabrics by the side just

before my mum left after I weaned my baby. Mum had found a way to tell me about the need to invest in another business idea because she knew how much I hated to hear about business when I was actively in paid employment.

Fast forward, I came in contact with a supplier and I ventured into foot wears. Prior to this time, in one of my moves to get my foodstuff one day, I met a woman who had been into the foodstuff business for years. She told me the nitty-gritty of the business even though it did not look like something I was interested in at the time. While in the middle of our conversation with another woman, who happened to be one of my primary school teachers, she heard me talk about my love for the fabric business and had great admiration for my expertise in business. She instantly said her daughter would be interested in my services. She gave me the daughter's contact and that was the beginning of a great business relationship between us.

She made her first bulk order of Ankara fabrics and I sold out in no time. She would buy from me and resell to her colleagues and friends. To keep up with her demands, I would skip lectures to go to my supplier and that was how the business continued to boom. I later proceeded to online marketing where I would display pictures of my fabrics on my social media handles and the result I got was remarkable so much that the orders I got daily were mind-blowing.

Along the line, people started approaching me for other things I was not doing. I started getting enquiry for bags, aso-oke and other fashion essentials. Basically, people wanted a one-stop shop. All of these and many more led to the KAYP that we all know today. It is amazing that the same KAYP FOODS I was not doing for a long time was a major fallback for me during the pandemic, as I had to re-introduce it. Amazingly enough, I became very sensitive to the immediate needs of the people. I knew what people wanted during the pandemic was not dress or shoes but food and that I projected ruthlessly. They needed something to ease off from boredom, so I was open-minded. I introduced fruits and veggies to them and these actually landed me some good gigs with my existing and prospective clients.

One of my very consistent and high-profile clients sent me this message recently: "Remi, I think you are good at this. Put it up for subscription after the pandemic and see how far you can go." Wow! That statement alone was a push for me. So, in retrospect, you never can tell who is watching. Only keep at what you are good at. Add more knowledge to it and do not stop learning, relearning and unlearning.

Take away: There is always a new territory to conquer. So, if you want to sustain the win you have today, and keep winning streak, one thing you must do is to recognize that even though you are content with that which you have, it is okay to aim for more and want to be more. One win is not enough to rest on your oars especially where there is room and opportunity for other wins and successes.

Life Lesson
37

I LOVE TO HELP

This is who I am. I was born for this. My name, Remilekun means "comfort" and that is exactly what I love to do. I love to help. It is not in any way a sign of weakness. As much as I love to help, I also know when to say no. When I am drawn to you, be sure you have someone loyal for a lifetime. Someone said I am very sacrificial. Yes, that is who I am. I see it in the little things I do. This passion made me start KAYP and Mind Shift Series Academy, my new baby. I created this platform to help people become who they were made to be.

Permit me to delve into the purpose for Mind Shift Series. It is a platform meant for men and women alike, struggling to navigate. Maybe you are stuck and you do not have an idea of what is next. You are presently at a point where you feel the need to navigate but you don't know how. I help you to discover, develop, identify and commercialize whatever solution you have. I also help you to see the possibility of moving from point A to B. Now, the best place to start is to ask yourself **what you are good at,** and **what exactly can you do? Also, you may need to ask yourself some of the questions below;**

- **What do you admire about your childhood experiences?**

- **Write down 10 things you are good at.**

- **Write down 10 things you do well.**

- **What were some of the things that people make positive comment about or something that stood out for you while growing up?**

Do you know that 80% of what we do is habits? It simply means that what you consistently do over a period of time, has the capacity to grow and become a force. Successful people believe that to achieve success or anything of value, you need to have a mindset that beliefs everything is possible. There are however dotted lines that may stand in-between. Your ability to connect with your dotted lines, gives you an edge over every other person.

What are dotted lines? Dotted lines are tangible things you need to connect you from where you are to where you need to be. For you, your dotted lines could be knowledge gap, for some it might be value added relationships and to some it might just be the need for mind mapping and get clarity of purpose.

How then do you connect these dotted lines? You need to sit down and put pen to paper. What areas do you have gaps? Write them down and reminiscence over them, whatever you discover, begin to take necessary steps/action. Taking action does not necessarily mean you are ready to execute, it's only a means to an end.

Finally, ask yourself, who do you have around that has or possess some of these values, then map out process on how to approach them one after the other. What you have achieved in doing this is that you are a few steps closer to the journey of self-discovery. These are many more is what Mind shift series Academy is set to achieve.

Take away: We inspire people by what we say and what we do. When inspiration is provided, desire is born and momentum is lent to the docile, timid and inactive. This is why the world flocks to the successful and the powerful, those who have made things happen for themselves and for others. We are influencers in different spheres of endeavors, therefore we must take our role more seriously by adding values to individual's lives and destinies.

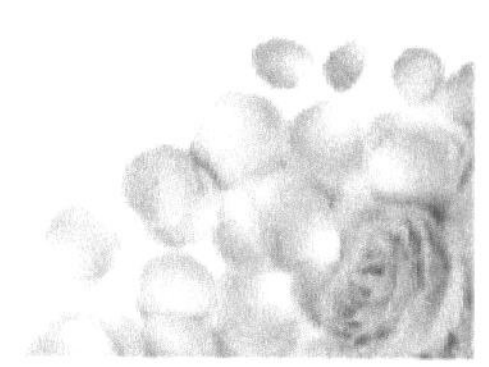

Life Lesson

38

THE GAME CHANGER

What can you do without God? Absolutely nothing! My Father is the Game Changer, the One who holds the universe in His hand; the Shekinah glory. He will give a promise and will see it come to fruition. I have not seen what He cannot do. The One who told 99-year-old Abraham in Genesis 17:1- 6 that "I am God Almighty, walk before me and be blameless... I will make you fruitful; I will make nations of you and kings will come from you." The Promise Keeper who always ensures every promise is kept. The One who leads by the still water. Our Keeper who neither sleeps nor slumbers. The very one who sees through our fears. The Almighty is His name. Our Shepherd who deliberately leads us through different phases of life. The One who restores us when we feel unacceptable.

Yes! I had to praise God there for a moment. He has always been at the center of my life. I could not have reached this milestone without Him.

Hallelujah!

Take away: First, God is a spiritual being, and when we say we are made in His image, it simply means we are also spiritual beings. You are a spirit, you possess a soul (the mind, will and emotions) and you live in a physical body. This here is the threefold nature of every person. We are primarily like God because of the spiritual part of us, which is the very core of who we are. What also makes us like Him is the fact that we can speak life-giving words, and we have authority on the earth. This puts us in a tremendously powerful position as individuals because it means we are not subject to all the negative things that may be going around us. We have the power to speak words that can change our situations and circumstances.

Culled from Authentic

Dare to be real by Taffi Dollars

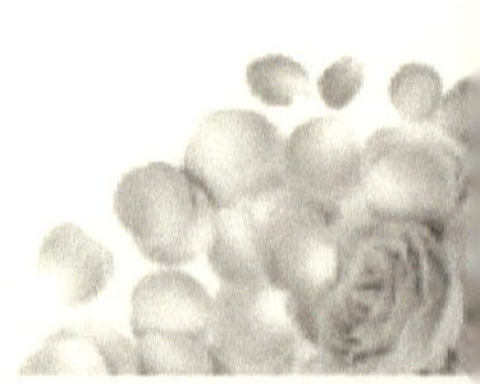

Life Lesson 39

THE NEW CHAPTER - TRANSITIONING

I was super active with school and church activities when I was much younger. You may ask why not more of academics than activities. My answer is that we all are wired differently and that does not negate the fact that I still did well in school. Perhaps, the One who created me knew the best fit for my frame and as such, He designed it to be so.

However, as I advanced in age, all my childhood strengths disappeared and I often wondered what happened. I totally lost interest in any form of activities. I became very timid, introverted and everything you can name with such temperament.

Whenever my mum told me to attend weddings and I declined because of my timidity, she would ask why I was shy when I was not the bride. Going defensive, I would tell her that everyone at the wedding would be looking at me. This always made her sigh. It was not until recently that I got my competencies back when life happened. It was like a rushing wind. So, if you ever see me with so much energy today, it has always been there. I just could not figure it all out then. It got worse when I was at the University of Jos, where I stayed with my uncle, Mr. Peter Oyeneye. He tried everything possible. On an occasion, he asked me to come out of my room and attend a particular meeting with some couples in attendance. While there, he asked me to share few tips about marriage to the couples in attendance. Amazingly enough, I was not thinking about marriage then. But then, I loved reading romantic novels and mostly Christian literature on marriage. I guess that was why he called me out in that gathering to speak. In the end, I concluded that all he was trying to do then was to help me become who I needed to be.

What more can I say? God is good and faithful to His Word. He says He will not withhold his covenant. Thank God for the grace to hold on and to do according to His will. This next phase of my life, eyes have not seen, nor have ears heard all that is ahead of me. It is a new decade, a new phase and a new season. I embrace it with so much elation in my heart.

Take away: God made you in His image and likeness. Therefore you can't afford to live life in small portion. Live your life like you are on a mission. Unleash your full potential.

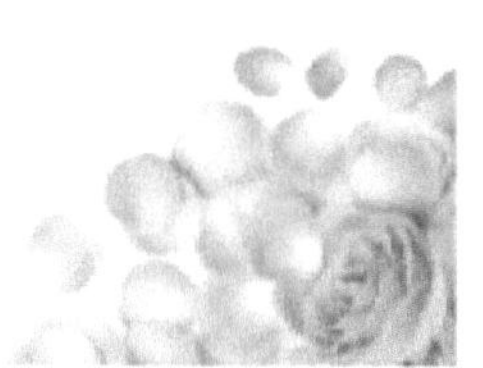

Life Lesson

40

NOW THAT I AM 40

There is more! Remi, launch into the fullness of all God has for you. Embrace the new as you part with the old. It is a new decade which I am mindful of. But then, when I count the many experiences, joy, pains and the uncertainties herein, I can only put them all in a whole. Forty seems to be opening me up to many new things which I need to do. Now is the time to explore and be more. Here comes the forty I have always looked forward to - the very one I prepared for and imagined many times.

Many things are yet to unfold. But through it all, God has given me many reasons to be grateful. When I think through it, all I see is God, His faithfulness, His sovereignty and all. He is the Father who does amazing things beyond our comprehension. Nobody can fathom His ways. His reasoning surpasses our imaginations. Still, He has chosen the foolish things of this world to confound the wise. I can only trust Him for what He has in store for me and my generation because faithful is HE that has promised.

Take away: Here is to an amazing decade. If you are below 40, mid or over 40, there is more to life than living for yourself or your immediate family. What counts the most is the kind of life that touches people around you positively. Life is not all about you, but about value and impact. Live positively and impact your world.

SHALOM!

Note from the author

Thank you for reading 40 Life Lessons!

I want to believe some of the lessons connect with you, irrespective of your journey.

Beyond reasonable doubt, I encourage you to own your journey. You are your best cheerleader, irrespective of some sort of external factors, believe you can become.

Be consistent and believe all will be well.

You can purchase this book as a gift for someone, your teenagers, your colleagues and friends. Read, recommend and review.

Thank you.

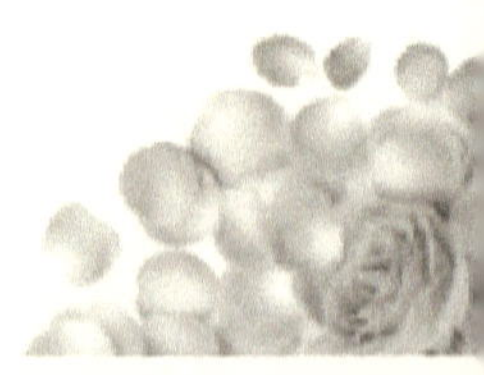

Mind Shift Series Academy

Mind Shift Series Academy is an online mentoring platform which helps you overcome the things that challenge you the most. Learn about personality type, strengths and weaknesses, mindset shifts, working through your emotions, taking care of your energy and connecting with your most authentic self.

I want to show you how to get clarity on your life's purpose and take action on it right now.

I will light a path forward to show you how doable it really is to live the life you imagine while serving others in the ways you feel most alive. In order to make brilliant things we need the courage to begin before we're "ready" or "perfect".

I find coaching so rewarding because I have helped some individuals find momentum and create a life they love waking up to.

I can't wait to see you in this course.

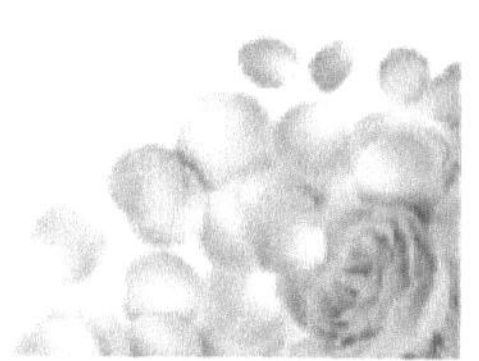

OUTCOMES

JOURNEY TO SELF DISCOVERY

BUSINESS IDEAS GENERATION

HOW TO START WITH LITTLE OR NO
CAPITAL

HOW TO START A DROP SHIPPING BUSINESS

HOW TO PACKAGE YOUR SKILLS AND KNOWLEDGE INTO
CREATIVE SERVICE YOU CAN SELL ONLINE

BUILDING YOUR OWN COMMUNITY

Welcome on board.

Remilekun Kehinde-Philip
Lead Coach
Mind Shift Series Academy(MSSA)
Lagos, Nigeria
Mindset shifts...

For more inquiry, please drop your details at
https://bit.ly/mindshiftseriesacademy

IDENTITY, DISCOVERY & EXECUTION MASTER CLASS

Mind Shift subscription based Master Class is for individuals who are ready to upskill and monetize their idea based knowledge gap.

MIND SHIFT

6 MONTHS
Subscription based

MIND SHIFT SERIES ACADEMY (MSSA)

Email : mindshiftseries@gmail.com

Enquiry: 07064416283, 08135016551

Medium : WhatsApp

Cost : #25,000

Renewable at expiration...

Connect with the author

You can connect with Remilekun at:

LinkedIn: Remilekun Kehinde-Philip

Facebook: Remilekun Kehinde-Philip

Twitter: @remilekuphilip

Instagram: www.instagram.com/kremilekun

Instagram: www.instagram.com/kayp_giftregistry

Instagram: www.instagram.com/kayp_wardrobe

Instagram: www.instagram.com/kayp_foods

Instagram: www.instagram.com/mindshift_series

For further inquiry on this book,
Please email: **mindshiftseries@gmail.com**